George Tierney

Substance of a Speech

delivered at a general court of proprietors, in Leadenhall-street, on

Wednesday, December 3, 1783

George Tierney

Substance of a Speech
delivered at a general court of proprietors, in Leadenhall-street, on Wednesday, December 3, 1783

ISBN/EAN: 9783337380274

Printed in Europe, USA, Canada, Australia, Japan

Cover: Foto ©Suzi / pixelio.de

More available books at **www.hansebooks.com**

SUBSTANCE

OF A

SPEECH

DELIVERED AT

A General Court of Proprietors,

In LEADENHALL-STREET,

On WEDNESDAY, December 3, 1783.

LONDON:

Printed for J. DEBRETT, (Succeſſor to Mr. Almon,)
oppoſite Burlington Houſe, Piccadilly.

MDCCLXXXIII.

TO THE RIGHT HONOURABLE

CHARLES JAMES FOX,

One of his Majesty's Principal Secretaries
of State.

Right Hon. Sir,

I AM encouraged to intrude myself
into your presence by that liberal and
just sentiment you have been pleased to
express—that you were anxious to be informed of all that could be said on the
subject of the East India Company's affairs, before you wished to carry the Bill,
now under the consideration of Parliament, into a Law.

Sir, the public prints have as entirely
misrepresented the debates carried on in
the Court of Proprietors, as they have
mutilated those of your Honourable
House. I will not do otherwise than pity
their manœuvres, because I am persuaded
that YOU *could have no design* in pre-
venting our deliberations from going out
into the world.—I therefore agree, that

this

this laſt contemptible meaſure is only a conſequence of that corruption you are ſo eager to remedy—It muſt be that Mr. Haſtings, from whom all modern iniquities proceed, has uſed his undue and ſhameful intereſt to prevent his Majeſty's ſubjects from knowing the ſentiments of each other.

Under theſe circumſtances, I hold it my duty to inform you, that the following Speech is what is reported by the papers in words to the following purpoſe : "Mr. Tierney called Mr. Moore to or-" der, and then made another *humorous* "*attack* on Mr. Fox." As the patron of wit, if wit I had made uſe of, I am convinced you would thank me for communicating it; but not being conſcious of all that *humour* attributed to me in ſo flattering a manner by the daily publications, I muſt take the liberty to lay before you what appear to me to be rather *ſerious conſiderations.*—That the meaſure propoſed DESTROYS PUBLIC CRE-DIT—VIOLATES THE KING's PRE-ROGA-

ROGATIVE,—and, to fay nothing more, goes near TO JUSTIFY AN INSUR-RECTION OF THE PEOPLE UPON THE PRINCIPLES YOU YOUR-SELF HAVE DEFENDED.

But, Sir, that I may not be accufed of mifreprefenting what I really did deliver, permit me to ftate the only ludierous part of my addrefs to the Proprietors. Fear-ful of having wearied them by rather too long an intrufion on their patience, I thought, in gratitude for their attention, I was called upon to revive their fpirits (if poffible, after the depreffion my dul-nefs muft have caufed) by fhewing, that though we were much abufed, yet that *the landed property of the kingdom* was not lefs duped. I therefore ventured, with all due fubmiffion, to infinuate that your mighty boaft of being enabled to avoid any additional tax on the country gentle-men by their fupport to the prefent Bill, might be, in fome degree, illuftrated by the following ftory.

A certain Wag, whofe wardrobe was reduced to great fcantinefs, went down to

a dif-

a diftant village to exercife his talents in
ways and means. " Good God !" fays
he, " my friends ! how awkward that
" CHURCH of yours ftands—let us pufh
" it into yonder field, and then it will
" be commodious for every body." The
clowns confented to the propofal, upon
condition that it fhould not be moved further than to *the edge of the 'Squire's ef-
tate*; and fo eager were they all upon
this new fcheme of improving the Pa-
rifh, that the only difficulty remaining
was, how they fhould know when to ftop.
" Put your coats down at a proper dif-
" tance," fays Scapin, " and I'll hollow
" to you when you come to them."—
Sir, the Simpletons fhoved with all their
might and main, till by fome accident or
other the Garments vanifhed——the fly
dog then cried out, " Hold, neighbours !
" Do you want to overturn the Church ?
" Why, you've pufhed it paft the mark,
" and *buried your own Clothes !*"

Take the India Houfe for the Church,
the parifhioners for the landed property, and the clothes for county intereft,
and

an d then, perhaps, in the circle of your acquaintance, you may be able to difcover *the wag.* Let the country gentlemen wheel about this *Leadenhall Church* wherever they pleafe; but I fhould caution them not to fhove too hard, for fear of overfhooting the mark. Perhaps, in a little time, they may hear the modern Scapin, (when he has gained his Ends, and wifhes again to appear a Patriot,) perhaps they may hear him bawl out, " Why, Gentlemen, what have you " done! You have pufhed the India " Houfe into the middle of Yorkfhire, " and crufhed your own Independence !" If they find any one in the county who will have fo much intereft as their new Vifitor, or who will difcover half fo excellent a choice in difcerning proper Members of Parliament, I will congratulate them on their acquifition.

Sir, I am aware that this may be called *low humour*; but, when I heard a certain great Man, in ftating the affairs of the firft trading Company in the world, on a fudden quit the fober path of calculation,

lation, and introduce *Falstaff's Tavern Bill* not being experienced in public oratory, I was led to conceive, that proving a fact, and raising a laugh, were the same thing; and that the importance of the subject was always supposed in an inverse proportion to the poorness of the jest. I am, however, convinced of my mistake; and on that account, in giving this speech to the public, I have left out every thing that might bear a ludicrous appearance.

I have therefore, Right Honourable Sir, only to pray you, that the mirth I was unlucky enough to inspire, may not be attributed to the Proprietors as *a new Crime*; and heartily wishing your Bill all the success it deserves, beg leave to subscribe myself,

Your most obedient,

humble servant,

GEORGE TIERNEY.

Lincoln's Inn,
Dec. 8th, 1783.

Subftance of a Speech, &c.

I RISE to fecond the motion of the Honourable Gentleman, and in doing this, I fhall
take the liberty to confider the Bill in queftion
at large.

Sir, I hold it beneath us to ufe the
little mean and paltry quibbles, which
have been adopted in another houfe; and
therefore I fhall not make any complaints, as
to our want of notice, though, at the fame
time I cannot help obferving, that had the
Honourable Secretary followed precedent, we
fhould have had timely information of the
matter in agitation. For in the year 1768,
when the Company had attracted the eye
of Government, the Firft Lord of the

B   Treafury,

Treafury, acting as became a Minifter, fent a meffage to the Court of Directors, dated September 24, informing them, " That as " the affairs of the Eaft India Company had " been mentioned in Parliament laft feffion, " it was very probable they might be taken " into confideration again ; therefore, from " the regard they had for the welfare of the " Company, and that they might have time " to prepare their papers for that occafion, " they informed them that the Parliament " would meet fome time in November." Of this precedent, I fay, I will take no advantage, but proceed to meet the queftion openly and fairly.

But there is one previous obfervation that feems to be neceffary, and it is this : Many gentlemen have conceived, that they could not do any effential harm in voting for the queftion, becaufe the Right Honourable Secretary fays, it is but an experiment to make trial of the efficacy of the Bill ; and to prove this, he ftates, that it fhall only have effect for fuch a number of years. Now this has deceived many who have looked no further than words; whereas in fact, it ought to be con-

ftrued

ftrued as a moſt conſummate piece of cunning, which, if carried into effect, will enable the Honourable Secretary, either to keep his place or to raiſe a formidable oppoſition to the Miniſtry that turns him out. For he argues thus : If I ſtay in power till the expiration of the term, it follows of courſe, I ſhall have ſufficient intereſt to renew the Bill ; and, if before that time, I am thrown out, I ſhall then have an handle for oppoſing the renewal, and only need ſay, that I am convinced my experiment has not ſucceeded,—that circumſtances are changed,—and uſe exactly the ſame language that Oppoſition originally did when I firſt propoſed the meaſure. We have a right to ſuppoſe that this will be the caſe, becauſe it has been once before; and Mr. Fox now urges the very arguments in favour of Government, which four years ago he preſſed againſt them. The truth, however, is, that if the Honourable Secretary has only taken the trouble to preſerve his notes, there are few ſides of any queſtion, which he is not, from univerſal practice, equally maſter of; but on *this*, ſhould it ſucceed, he will certainly ſhine with additional and unuſual brilliancy.

Sir,

Sir, I now proceed to meet the Bill, on a footing, which it never yet has ftood upon. I will not quibble on words, or perplex with figures: if the Bill can ftand on the broad bafis it points to, it fhall have my moft cordial fupport; but I think I can overturn its very foundation.

I pledge myfelf to prove, that the Bill is not only *unneceffary*, but that even, fuppofing the evil to exift, the *remedy is inadequate:* and as it is on the reverfe of thefe two grounds that Miniftry fupport their arguments, they cannot fay I have evaded a fair combat.

Firft, then, I have engaged myfelf to prove that the Bill is *unneceffary,* and therefore it will be required from me, that I fhould feparately anfwer the two great arguments of our opponent. Firft, that we are *bankrupts;* and next, that *the Directors have proved themfelves infufficient.*

The Honourable Secretary, in making his original motion to the Houfe, laid it down as a leading pofition, that the Company were in a ftate of utter bankruptcy. The Directors

tors took the alarm at such an unexpected
assertion, and prepared "a state of their
"affairs" for the perusal of the public. This
Mr. Fox declared to be fallacious, and, in
about three quarters of an hour, so ably
twisted and turned the separate figures in each
article, that he convinced 229 members the
whole was false and ridiculous.

Now, Sir, it may be expected that, to
wipe off this disgraceful defeat, we should
answer as specifically as we are attacked—that
we should defend and explain every distinct
head of debt or credit. This I will hereafter
shew we are by no means called upon to do,
and, for the present, only say, that *I* have
not presumption enough to conceive myself
equal to the task. Had I indeed the abilities
of the Hon. Secretary, I, like him, would attempt any thing; for do but mark the force of
superior talents.—Mr. Fox, in three quarters
of an hour, can go through, explain, and
confute a commercial account, which, by his
own declaration, four and twenty merchants
are not even able to state: he can, such are his
astonishing powers, in one speech, make the
country gentlemen (who, whatever their other
merits

merits may be, certainly are not celebrated for calculation) comprehend the whole affairs of the greateſt trading Company in the world for years *paſt* and *years to come.* Why, Sir, throw away your *Wingates, Cockers,* and all the idle books we have been accuſtomed to look upon as arithmetical goſpel. Give me the new work, " Every Miniſter his own " Merchant, or the ſhorter Way of Subtrac- " tion."—Give me the rule of Seven to go by—no need of dividing and ſub-dividing— take all from all and what remains? Seven.— If I can't manage twenty-four Directors, how many can I? Seven.—If *I* can manage Seven, how many underſtrappers can they deal with? Eight!—This, Sir, ſeems to be the modern arithmetic; but as unfortunately I am not poſ- feſſed of this new work, I muſt content my- ſelf with conſidering certain of Mr. Fox's objections in a general manner.

Having produced our ſtatement to do away the charge of bankruptcy, the Hon. Secre- tary aſſerts it to be fallacious, " becauſe," ſays he, " ſome of the debts which you have put " down on the credit ſide *I don't believe* will be " paid." Why not? " Becauſe part of it is due " from

" from Government ; and " know all men by
thefe prefents, " that's not good for much."
·Now, a man would think this was rather an odd
declaration for a Minifter to make, who even
profeffed to have any regard for the credit of
his country ; but in the next article the Hon.
Secretary gives fome confolation, by affuring
us " that France is as bad as ourfelves : "
" the debt for fubfiftence of prifoners, &c.
" I am fure you never will touch, becaufe "
(now, as Mr. Fox faid by one of our notes,
what does any man think would follow ?)
" *becaufe the Embaffador at Paris is doing all*
" *be can to get it.*"

Then he goes on : " Some of this debt is due
" by Afoph ul Dowlah, and *be* can't pay you."
Why not ? "Becaufe *be fays fo.*" Well, but
can't we force him? "Aye," fays the noble Lord
in the blue ribband, " but then you'll burn
" villages, and all the world knows that's my
" averfion."—Sir, I muft own that it appears
a little extraordinary, to hear the noble Lord
come out with this fentiment, unlefs it be, that,
among the other bleffings of the Coalition,
Mr. F— hath incorporated fome of his ten-
dernefs into the breaft of his now gentle col-
league ;

league; for there are thofe who fay, that, for
eleven years together, this new-adopted fon
of mercy did not only caufe the burning and
facking of a few towns, but ftirred up and
conducted a moft unnatural war, between pa-
rents and their own children. But *now a
legal right* is to be given up, rather than put
an Indian chief to the fmalleft inconvenience—
fo " ftrike off that article, and let us proceed
" to your warehoufes and dead ftock :—thefe
" you fhan't give yourfelf credit for, nor ftate
" as a part of your effects." And yet the proof
that thefe are not to be confidered as our own,
is rather an *unufual* one. " If this Bill does
" not pafs, *an extent* muft iffue from the Trea-
" fury." An extent on what? Why, *on the very property we wont allow you to call your own.*

Sir, in this ftyle did the Hon. Secretary
proceed, till it appeared to the Houfe, *as*
CLEAR AS COULD BE, *that we were
bankrupts,* and that it would be *mercy* * to
manage our affairs for us.

---

* Mr. Fox feems to conftrue Shakefpeare literally;
where, fpeaking of the quality of mercy, he fays " it
" is twice bleffed; it bleffes him that gives, and him
" that *takes.*"

But

But, Sir, I faid that we were not obliged
to anfwer for every feparate article; neither are
we, until it fhall be fhewn by what right our
affairs are enquired into by Government. The
only reply that can be made. is, " You owe
" more than you can pay." " Well, but how
" much do we owe *you* ?" Exactly 1,741,254 l.
We anfwer, " Here is by cafh, bonds, deben.
" tures, and cuftom notes, 609,954; here is
" 400,000, being the remainder of the Pro-
" prietors original fubfcription ; and here are
" goods which have been allowed to be worth
" 2,500,000. Out of thefe we will fell to the
" amount of the fum required,(unlefs a feizure
" fhould be more agreeable to you,) and now
" you have no further claim upon us." Surely,
Sir, this is a fair mode of arguing with any
moderate men ; but, alas ! government are
bent on our ruin; and therefore, not content with being paid all that is due to *themfelves*, they infift upon our proving that we
are able to pay our *other creditors* at the
fame fhort notice. Sir, is this a Houfe of
Commons or an Inquifition !—Might we not
juftly fay, By what right do you put our
credit to the torture ? are there any clamorous
creditors at our doors ? is any man urgent

for

for payment? have we denied ourſelves, or attempted any ſuſpicious evaſions? I defy the Honourable Secretary to ſay it; and more, I maintain in his teeth, that the Law of England is violated by a proceeding which authorizes a creditor, *after being ſatisfied*, to ſtigmatize and injure the reputation of his debtor; and I do aſſert, that the conduct of Parliament is ſuch, as in an individual would be actionable, and that too for one of the meaneſt offences known againſt the peace of ſociety. But what cares the Miniſter? Callous to the public hooting, he perſiſts in his bold ſcheme, and dares to ſay, " Prove *now* that " you, a commercial Company, having exten- " ſive ventures at ſea, can pay all your creditors " at a moment's notice, and diſcharge debts " which will not become due till the year " 1786, or we will ſeize your every thing." Why, the Honourable Secretary is worſe than Shylock. Shylock waited till his bond became due; Shylock *then* aſked no more than his pound of fleſh; but Government would ſeize the whole body even before they have a right to mangle a limb— Gracious God! only mark in the gradatior of human iniquity, how much more mc

dera'

derate is the favage hunger of an unnatural
Jew, than the avarice of a rapacious Minifter !

But, Sir, let us not bear this ! We have
been infulted, and let us revenge ourfelves !
let us publifh our memorial to the world, and
fay, " Judge if our refentment be not jufti-
" fiable. Our Country hath fpurned and
" trampled upon *us*; what duty then owe
" we to *our country?* We fupported
" her in the hour of danger, and voluntarily
" involved *ourfelves* in difficulties to fave *her*
" from difgrace;—we gave her fhips to
" ftrengthen her forces; and at the very mo-
" ment of her drooping, cheer'd her with the
" feafonable relief; and how hath fhe rewarded
" us? By making the very debts we incur-
" red in her fupport, one of the pretences
" for feizing our Franchifes and Charter—
" Away with moderation ! All ties of affec-
" tion, of relationfhip, are at an end ; and
" neceffity compels us to retort on the un-
" grateful cruelty of her behaviour. PAY
" US FOUR MILLIONS, FOR YOU
" OWE IT ! Prove that you are able to
" difcharge your debt on the inftant, or by

" your

" your own raſh declaration YOU are *BANK-*
" *RUPTS.* Let the whole world be witneſs,
" that we only do as we have been done by ;
" and if we involve our Country in ruin, we
" have not acted but on the moſt daring
" provocation."—Sir, would not this, though
ſtern, be juſtifiable language? And ought
not every honeſt man to curſe the meaſure
that could drive us to theſe extremities? But
let not our aſſailants be diſmayed ; I truſt
that we deſpiſe them too much to retaliate.
No! we will ſhew the world how Engliſh-
men ought to act, and prove that the very
Company they aim to correct, is capable of
reading them the moſt humiliating leſſon on
their conduct. *We* will not ſeek for a little
pecuniary gratification, by diſtreſſing fellow-
ſubjects, much leſs an important national
concern. *We* will not urge the payment of a
debt, which would affect the credit of our
Conſtitution.—No, Sir! we will learn from
our enemies the degrading impolicy and
wickedneſs of ſuch ill-timed avarice, and
teach theſe ſhallow reformers the duty of Ci-
tizens.—And now, if the Honourable Secretary have a bluſh remaining, let him ſhew
ſigns of Grace.

Sir,

Sir, on this head, I truft, I have fufficiently demonftrated, that we are not quite
in a ftate of bankruptcy, unlefs that merchant is, *who can pay all that is due to the
only creditor who demands*; but who cannot, on a fudden notice, advance the cafh for
what *is not yet due*; and to this I may add,
that we are not Bankrupts according to the
ftate of Englifh funds, as long as an hundred
pounds Eaft India Stock will fell for an hundred and twenty. Proceed we therefore to the
next reafon affigned for this Bill; and that is,

" THE NEGLECT OF THE DIRECTORS."

Sir, the crime imputed to the Gentlemen
in the Direction, both by the words of the Bill,
and of Mr. Fox's Speech, is, that they have
neglected to examine the charges tranfmitted
to them againft their fervants abroad, and
neither recalled or ordered profecutions againft
perfons fo charged, even where on examination
the cafe hath appeared to require fuch feveri-
ty; and alfo that they have fuffered many grofs
inftances of wilful and contumacious difobe-
dience, to pafs either without examination,
or without a confequent recall or punifhment,
whereby,

whereby, says the great mover of the Act, servants have become greater than their masters.

Sir, this is so very vague and unsupported an insinuation, that I am persuaded Government itself never could seriously look for an answer to it; neither, till the accusation be more substantiated, is it possible to make any sort of reply : but yet the terms are too choice to be past over in silence, and I trust I shall be forgiven, if I wander some little from the question, in order, if I can, to illustrate this very curious preamble.

As to servants being greater than their masters, I do allow it to be a most dangerous offence, and hence it is that I cannot place any confidence in those men who strained it to the highest degree ever known, and suffered the kingdom to remain six weeks without any government, rather than allow their Royal Master his established prerogative of chusing his own ministers. I do, therefore, most heartily thank the Honourable Secretary for the abhorrence he testifies of this shameful behaviour, and as, to be sure, neither he, or any of his friends, can find themselves in the smallest degree galled by a crime they are so anxious to punish, I take

this

this opportunity, for once, to coincide with them, and to declare this the moſt dangerous and inſolent miſdemeanour I know of.

Indeed, I am perfectly of opinion with the Honourable Secretary in the whole of this preamble, and therefore I ſhould humbly move him, that the Houſe of Commons be in future managed by ſeven Commiſſioners. The ſame form of accuſation will do ; only, for variety, we will more ſpecifically deſcribe the tranſgreſſion : " Whereas it appears, that, " for about eight years, the Right Honourable " Charles Fox did little elſe than accuſe and " lay charges againſt the Right Honourable " Lord North, nay ſtated him to be ſo utterly in- " capable of performing his duty as a Miniſter, " and ſo very dangerous in his principles as a " man, that the ſaid Charles Fox declared him " unfit to hold the reins of government, and " proteſted he ſhould not care to truſt himſelf " an hour in the ſame room with him ; there- " fore, to the intent that good management be " reſtored, be it enacted, that ſeven commiſ- " ſioners be conſtituted to examine into this " grievance, and that the ſaid Charles Fox be " called upon to make good his accuſations."

This

This is one bill I would propose to the Honourable Secretary ; but as it would be a pity so happy and juft a turn of thinking as he hath here expreffed fhould not be made the moft of, and as I am fure his wonted candour and liberality will thank me for any hints of reform I can point out, I will beg leave to propofe another act on the fame principle. " Whereas it appears that cer-
" tain charges of unjuft and fraudulent prac-
" tices have been prefented againft two clerks
" in the Paymafter's office, and it further
" appears that the Paymafter not only refufed
" to remove the faid clerks, but even de-
" fended them in their wrong doing, and ne-
" ver examined into the matter coolly, but
" loft all temper whenever the fubject was
" mentioned ; and whereas it fhould feem
" that a charge coming from the Lords of
" his Majefty's Treafury deferved more de-
" ference and refpect, therefore be it enacted,
" that feven Commiffioners be appointed for
" managing the affairs of the Paymafter's
" office, and that the Right Honourable
" Paymafter be immediately compelled to
" furrender all books, papers, &c. belonging
" to the faid office."

But,

But, Sir, all raillery apart, I faid I would prove the Bill perfectly unneceffary; and I do not in the fmalleft degree wifh to wave my promife. As to our bankruptcy, I truft I have fufficiently fhewn the cruelty, danger, and futility of that plan; and therefore what I now conceive myfelf called upon to do, is to point out that *regulation* would have been fufficient for every evil complained of.

I take it there is a diftinction to be made where the caufe of mifchief is afcertained, and where not. In one cafe (where we only find by experience that things go wrong), fome new mode muft be adopted; but in the other, where we difcover the reafon of the mifchief, regulation and amendment is all that is wanted. To inftance this, take the late act for appointing Commiffioners of public Accounts: it recites that great lofs had arifen to the public from the prefent inconvenience in accounting for the receipts, iffues, and expenditure of certain monies; therefore it enacts, that Commiffioners fhall be appointed for confidering of and reporting by what means and methods the public

D   accounts

accounts may in future be paffed in a
more expeditious and effectual manner.
To this Bill no objection of confequence was
made ; but had it ftated, that *the caufe* of the
delay and inconvenience arofe from the accountants in the different offices neglecting
to examine the accounts prefented to them,
and that therefore feven Commiffioners
fhould be appointed to manage the affairs of
all the public offices in the kingdo.n, furely
the cafe would have been different. Every
man would have faid, Why give thefe feven
new men the power of naming clerks with
high falaries, and the influence that power
muft naturally bring with it, when the remedy is fo very fimple and obvious, which
will keep matters in the old channel ? Only
make the accountants more refponfible, and
the punifhment for the breach more than a
counterbalance for any reward they can receive for overlooking the duties of their
ftation. Similar to this I take is our cafe :
the caufe is declared to be *the neglect
of the Directors in not examining into
the charges tranfmitted againft their fervants abroad*, and, to my apprehenfion,
this carries on the very face of it the mode
of

of remedy required: it is but lodging a greater degree of refponfibility in the Directors, and heightening the punifhment for overlooking offences. Sir, I am the more ftrengthened in this argument, becaufe I have never yet heard imbecillity imputed to the managers of the India Company ; nay, the refolution of the Houfe of Commons holds fo very contrary a language, that their orders are cited as being a mafterly fyftem of ethics. The only reafon, therefore, that could poffibly be urged againft me fails ; and I do conceive myfelf, even in this ftage of my argument, warranted in laying it down, that the *prefent Bill is unneceffary, becaufe there is no evil complained of, which fimple regulation would not remove.* However, I need not reft it here, as the confideration of the Bill itfelf will, I truft, give additional ftrength to what I have ventured to premife.

THE BILL IS INCOMPETENT.

Sir, I have before ftated what the mifchief was the act in queftion profeffed to remedy : it remains now to proceed with the latter half of the great claufe in page 7. " Be " it enacted, that, whenever any charge of cor-

" ruption,

" ruption, peculation, oppreffion, extortion,
" receipt of prefents, ufury, breach of orders,
" or other grievous offence, fhall be exhibited
" before the Governor-general and Council of
" Bengal, or the Prefident and Council of any
" of the Prefidencies or fettlements abroad,
" and tranfmitted to the Court of Directors,
" hereby difcontinued, or to the faid Commif-
" fioners, againft any of the Governors, Pre-
" fidents, or Members of the Council, civil
" or military, in the Company's fervice ; or
" which fhall be exhibited by any of the native
" Princes; and the faid Commiffioners fhall
" within   after the fame fhall be made,
" examine into fuch charge: and if, upon
" examination, they fhall not think proper
" either to recall or order a profecution, every
" Commiffioner, making fuch examination,
" *fhall enter in writing, in the Journals,* his opi-
" nion on the validity and importance of fuch
" charge, with his fpecific reafons, on the par-
" ticular cafe, for not recalling the perfon, or
" ordering a profecution."

This, Sir, is the remedy this great and all-pro-
vident Bill propofes; this is the important regulation for which the Minifter is to be rewarded
                                            with

with unbounded patronage, and the chartered
rights of a great Company are to be deftroyed.
A mighty regulation truly! Either you, the
new Commiffioners, fhall redrefs all grievances, or elfe *you fhall give your reafons
for not doing fo.* Is there any thing here
which the prefent Directors are not capable of
performing, as well as the moft fagacious of
Mr. Fox's friends? Is there any thing here
which might not have been introduced without a violation of the Company's very conftitution? Nothing! Only let it be granted
that the Directors can *write Englijh,* and this
Bill is *perfectly ufelefs.*—I do not conceive
myfelf called upon to enter into any one other
claufe of the Bill: this is the whole of the
remedy; nor can any man fhew me a fingle
fyllable which holds out an additional advantage to the Company's affairs. The only fecurity which could render this Act any thing
like an important regulation, would be ftating fome fevere punifhment, in cafe by the
Journals it fhould appear, that the Commiffioners, in not examining into charges, had
acted wrong. But what's the confequence of
mifbehaviour to be? Why, that it fhall be
lawful for his Majefty to remove any of the
faid

said Commissioners, upon an address of either House of Parliament. Now, Sir, do but see what a shallow security we have for their honesty. If they have a majority upon the mere prospect of the power that is to be given them, is it reasonable to suppose they will be deserted, because they have the actual possession of it ? I feel that gratitude is not much the fashion; but I will not have so very bad an opinion of the Honourable Secretary's party, as to suppose they will forsake men, merely because they are under obligations to them.

Sir, from all that I have said, may I not venture to assert, that the Bill is unnecessary ?

First, Because we are not in such a State of Bankruptcy as to warrant this attack on our Charter ; unless he is a Bankrupt, who can pay the only creditor that makes a demand upon him.

Secondly, Because there is an obvious remedy deducible from a cause admitted, which would answer every purpose that the Bill itself in its own words requires.

'And

And that the Bill is incompetent, I trust is plain, because it does not give any additional security for the future abolition of those evils and mischiefs which it professes to remedy.

Sir, I will only make an obfervation on one or two of the claufes, and then proceed to canvafs the Bill fairly, and on broad grounds as to its *general tendency.*

The Eight Affiftant Directors feem to me to poffefs the moft extraordinary place that I believe was ever yet invented; they are ftated to be chofen and appointed for the *fole purpofe of managing the Commerce* of the Company, and therefore *they are required to purfue fuch orders as they fhall receive from the Commiffioners, who are not appointed to manage the Commerce.* If the Honourable Secretary could ftoop to explanation, I fhould be glad to know what is meant by men having the management of a thing which others are to direct?

The other claufe on which I fhall obferve, is that which watches with fuch jealous

care

care over the property and perfon of all Indian
Princes. I cannot, Sir, but remark, that it is
forcing us to make rather a degrading comparifon to confider the lenity and juftice fhewn
to the natives of India, and the difference
of treatment which *we* experience. When I
began to read the Bill, I pitied the Honourable Secretary, as a man who did not feem to
have the moft diftant idea of what equity
was; but on coming to this part, I found
that the infult he has been pleafed to offer to
the cuftom of his Country is abfolutely wan-
ton. It appears now, that he does know,
that, to come at the truth, it is neceffary not
only *to hear every material article, or head of*
charge ; but alfo to *examine into it fpecifically,*
and not generally and in grofs. Mr. Harding
quoted the Pfalms, and faid, " Oh ! that mine
" enemy had done me this wrong !" but I
cannot help exclaiming, " Oh ! that I were
" an Indian Prince ! for then I fhould not
" have had my property taken from me,
" without having a regular charge produced,
" and having that charge regularly examined
" into ;" but being, as I am, a mere Englifh
fubject, the Honourable Secretary chufes to
condemn

condemn me unheard, and as he himfelf emphatically ftyles it, " *in Grofs.*"

Sir, I merely obferve on this claufe to prove how very unneceffary it would be to go thro' the others. We are clearly fhewn by the mode of proceeding adopted againft us, that it is not meant to give us juftice : I otherwife, perhaps, might have gone on to prove, that the balance of advantage to the Company ftands with the prefent eftablifhment, becaufe the Directors are amenable to the King's Bench;— a much more fummary method than waiting for an addrefs to the King; for which, not being a member of Parliament, I, though a Proprietor, never can move. I might, perhaps, have gone on to ftate that I did not find in the Bill any one profpect of ever receiving another dividend, or any opportunity I fhould in future have of transferring, without the fpecial voluntary permiffion of thefe feven demi-gods. But all this is now ufelefs. The fentence is paft before the culprit is heard; and I muft kifs the rod in filence, unlefs I can fhew, that this Act is enough to rouze the whole kingdom by it's

E GENERAL

GENERAL TENDENCY.

Sir, This is a meafure which not only affects the Eaft India Company, but ftrikes at the very fundamental bafis of the conftitution. The precedent once eftablifhed, I know of no man whofe property is fecure ; I know of no Corporation whofe exiftence I would warrant for a fingle hour; nor do I know of any Act of Parliament in which I can confide. As long as the plunder of the Eaft will ftay the appetites of ambitious hunger, the *Bank* of *England* may be fecure—no longer. While the fpoils of our Company will fate thefe fons of rapine, the great chartered Bodies of the kingdom, may breathe awhile—but the axe muft fall fometime. As long as the prefent booty lafts, an Act of Parliament may be almoft as good as a Minifter's opinion—but there's the boundary. Sir, I would fain fhew the world, in gentle language, that this is a moft dangerous precedent ; and, if poffible, prevail on Government to give it up: but the cafe is too defperate to be trifled with ; and therefore, how dreadful foever the profpect, it is the duty of every honeft man to view it.——THE KING IS A CORPORATION, AND HIS FAMILY ARE ONLY SETTLED BY AN ACT OF PAR-

PARLIAMENT.——Let every loyal fubject look to it, for I fay again, the precedent is *dangerous* and *alarming*.

This is a meafure which DESTROYS
THE PUBLIC CREDIT.

Sir, if ever there was a cruel ftab wantonly
given to the credit of a country, it was,
when the Honourable Secretary was pleafed,
in his capacity of Minifter, openly to declare,
that the creditors of the nation were always
for the future, in ftating their affairs, to
reckon the debt, due by Great Britain, as
only worth four fifths of the original loan.

I did, Sir, flatter myfelf, and fo muft many
others have done, that at leaft the appearance of honefty would have been preferved,
and that no man would be found daring
enough to deftroy even the *fiction* of *fecurity*.——
It is in vain, however, to reflect, for the
blow *is ftruck*; and all we now can do is, to
fubmit, in mortifying filence, to what every
foreigner may taunt us with. They will begin
to draw comparifons between their government
and ours, which, till now, would have been
honourable to England, but after this Bill
has paffed, they will fay, that it favours ex-

actly

actly of the meafures purfued in their own
country *in what is bad*, and does not imitate
them in *what is good*, even though the ex-
ample be recent. Aye, and they may illuf-
trate their fatire.

Sir, it is a melancholy reflection, that the
inftance moft fimilar to this act of our Legiflature, is to be found in an abfolute and un-
controuled government. I mean the fup-
preffion of the Jefuits in France; where a
whole fociety, without any one criminal charge
openly alledged againft them, were, in one
night, deprived of all their employments;
had all their property confifcated, and found
themfelves turned out into the world under
the fevereft odium of guilt :—but the mercy
of heaven is infinite, and the day of retri-
bution feems at hand, when the Jefuit fhall
tyrannize in his turn!

Sir, if this *fimilarity* in oppreffion prefent a chilling profpect, what fhall we fay
to the *contraft* which France can hold up to
us,—a contraft that muft raife a blufh in
the moft abandoned of our Rulers. I al-
lude to the failure of the Caiffe d'Efcompte,

or

or Paris Bank, which will ſhew us that Eng-
liſh ſpirit is lowered indeed, and read a degrading leſſon to the profeſſors of modern
patriotiſm.

This failure of the Caiſſe d'Eſcompte
was an abſolute one : the Company were not
merely ſtated to be Bankrupts in a crafty
ſpeech, but actually confeſſed themſelves una-
ble to diſcharge a ſingle ſhilling. Under theſe
circumſtances what does an abſolute Monarch ? And what does the prime Miniſter
of a Sovereign without controul advise ? *To
support the Company who were eſtabliſhed
under the protection of the King ; to allow them
time to ſettle and arrange their affairs, and ſtrain
the point of authority, rather to defend than de-
ſtroy the reputation of a chartered body.* This
comes from Slaves! This is the way in which
Bondſmen proceed, while we that boaſt of
our Liberty, and hold ourſelves up as models
of Freedom, ſuffer a Miniſter to propoſe a
meaſure which even deſpotiſm diſavows!
Why, Sir, the French have ſhewn wiſdom and
liberal policy in their conduct. "We will not,"
ſay they, " paint our great commercial Com-
" panies in the colours of Bankruptcy; but ra-
" ther

" ther feek to glofs over, and conceal their mif-
" fortunes. Sooner let an hundred individuals
" fuffer, than the credit of an important national
" depofit of wealth be blown upon." So reafons
what we idly term Defpotifm: but in this land
of mock Liberty, how do we argue ? "Why, let
" Trade, Commerce, and national Faith, fink
" and fade to nothing, fome great man may,
" perhaps, be found bold and bad enough to fay
" —Let them rot and die, fo that I and my
" friends get places.—Yield me your Charter,
" tho' it blaft the reputation of your Country,
" for I have feven trufty ones to provide for !"

So much for the commercial principle of
this Bill. Let us next look to

THE LEGALITY OF THE ATTEMPT.

Sir, the ground on which the Honourable Secretary attempted to argue the pro-
priety of this act, was fuch an one as muft
make every honeft man fhudder. There is,
fays he, *a necessity superior to law which makes
this Bill legal.*   He deferves ill of his Country, who propofes meafures which force us to
deliver our opinions on fubjects which loyalty

ty would wifh to turn from; but I fhould.
deferve worfe, could I, having undertaken to
canvafs the fubject, fuffer fuch a daring plea
to pafs without an anfwer. I do agree, that
there is *a neceffity fuperior to law*; and I will,
fince I am driven to it, declare when it takes
place.

Sir, I infift that hiftory and pofitive law
both agree, that this neceffity can only prevail where fome violence is offered, for which
the Legiflature of the country hath provided
no remedy; and I readily join with the Honourable Secretary, that the Revolution is
an argument in point. May God and his
King forgive him, for what he hath done!
but only mark the principle of our Conftitution, to which his wicked rafhnefs hath
forced us to turn our eyes! I affert, that, in
the prefent cafe, no evil fubfifts which au-
thorifes the fmalleft deviation from the eftablifhed ufages of the Englifh Government.
Stand forward, Right Honourable Secretary,
for you did fay that fuch a mifchief did
fubfift. Now, Sir, either you or I muft
fall——the queftion is certainly brought to
a fair iffue. *Was the Revolution fuch an in-*
ftance

*stance of neceffity as to authorize and give
a precedent for the Bill in queftion?* I anfwer, No! and call as my evidence the late
Judge Blackftone. " The true principle
" upon which that memorable event pro-
" ceeded," fays my refpected witnefs, " was
" an entirely *new cafe* in Politics. The ab-
" dication of the reigning Monarch, and the
" vacancy of the Throne thereupon. It was
" the act of the nation alone upon a convic-
" tion that there was no King in being ; and
" the Lords and Commons in full conven-
" tion determined, that King James the Se-
" cond, having endeavoured to fubvert the
" Conftitution of the Kingdom, by breaking
" the original contract between King and peo-
" ple, and by the advice of Jefuits, and other
" wicked perfons, having violated the funda-
" mental law, and having withdrawn himfelf
" out of the Kingdom, has abdicated the
" Government, and that the Throne is there-
" by vacant. The Facts themfelves thus ap-
" pealed to, it belonged to our anceftors to
" determine ; for, whenever a queftion arifes
" between the Society at large and any ma-
" giftrate vefted with power originally dele-
" gated

" gated by that fociety, it muft be decided by
" the voice of the fociety itfelf ;—there is not
" upon earth any other tribunal to refort to"

Does the Right Honourable Secretary find
any fimilitude in this to warrant his prefent
attempt ? Can all his boafted eloquence point
out a fingle feature of comparifon to juftify
him ? Is a company of Merchants, neglecting to enquire into the mifmanagement of
their fervants, a fimilar inftance with the
vacancy of the Throne ? Or will the Minifter
be bare-faced enough to fay, that abufe of
power is *a new cafe in Politics* ? And yet he
muft prove all this, and ten times more, to
vindicate himfelf in his affertion.

Sir, was the attack now made merely againft
myfelf, I might, perhaps, ftop here, without
pufhing my advantage ; but, as I confider
myfelf pleading a public caufe, my duty calls
upon me to proceed. It is not fufficient to
have proved, that the inftance of the Revolution does not touch us ; but fince the Honourable Secretary hath unadvifedly thought
proper to turn our thoughts to the dangerous chapter in ours, and every Government,
he muft be told the *refult* of what we read—

let

let the confequences fall upon himfelf, becaufe, when he fhall have obtained the King's
affent to this Bill, it might perhaps be as
well, if he had not put the refolution of the
Convention in 1688 into our hands.

When men are reading the dreadful effects of " *violating the fundamental Laws*,"
may it not be rather dangerous to tell them,
that the facred rights of a Charter are deftroyed ? When we are intent on examining
into the mode of redrefs, in the cafe of an
endeavour to *fubvert the Conftitution*, is it
quite politic to let us fee that forfeiture is
incurred without accufation or trial? I fhould
think not—The fool may chance to mifun-
derftand the letter of legal diftinction ;—the
factious and violent, to ftrain it to a rafh
purpofe ; and the fteady Patriot, to read and
apply the inftruction. The calm fobriety of
clofet deliberation hath gone as far as to fay*,
that, to preferve our rights and liberties, when
actually violated or attacked, every Eng-
lifhman is intitled, in the firft place, " to
" the regular adminiftration and free courfe
" of

* Blackftone, ift vol. page 144.

" of juftice in the Courts of Law—next to the
" right of petitioning the King and Parlia-
" ment for redrefs of grievances—and laftly
" to the right of having and ufing arms for
" felf-prefervation and defence."—Perhaps
the moderation of Theory may be quickened
by a provocation to the vigour of Practice,
and the Honourable Secretary may find too
late, that the comment on the text is, *defperate Refiftance.* I beg pardon, Sir, for
ufing fuch language; but I truft no man
will mifconftrue my motives.——What I
lay down is only to fhew, how dangeroufly
wicked it is to propofe meafures which muft
tend to turn the minds of the people to ob-
jects which every honeft man would wifh
fhould remain buried in oblivion.

Sir, if there be ftill an argument wanting
to prove the very dangerous tendency of this
Bill, it will be found in confidering that

IT ATTACKS THE KING'S PREROGATIVE.

If I rightly comprehend the nature of
the conftitution I live in, I take certain privileges thrown into the fcale of the *execu-*
F 2   *tive,*

tive, to be intended as a balance or equipoise to the weight and influence of the *legiflative power*, and amongft thefe privileges or pre-rogatives, I imagine none to be more im-portant than that which declares the King the *Fountain of Honours*, and to have the right of *erecting and difpofing of offices.* Now, what does this Bill ? It deftroys them both ; for can any man be fo blind as not to fee the confequences that will arife from the meafure in agitation ? Is it not plain that our gracious Monarch will no longer be able to preferve the counterbalance which *Ambition* oppofes to *Intereft ?* Our fage forefathers, wifely ftudying the bias of humanity, found pride to be the only check againft avarice. They faw that there was a fomething in the word Title which dazzled the weak, ftimu-lated the brave, and which Wifdom herfelf felt gave folemnity to her meafures. The King was therefore made the fountain of Honour and Titles, that the Sovereign, when infulted, might, by the flattering diftinctions of preeminence, allure thofe to loyalty who were otherwife open to the bribery of the wealthy traitor. If this prerogative was when our anceftors founded the conftitutional fabric

only

only deemed a fufficient barrier againft the influence of this little ifland, what fhall become of it now? Corruption will meet no opponent; the treafures of the Eaft are thrown open to her difpofal; and Power (dreffed in the high-founding titles of Afiatic pomp) is proclaimed by the heralds of Venality to the mercenary troops of Faction. In vain may the forfaken Monarch hold out the plain infignia and modeft ermine of domeftic honours—the trappings of royalty itfelf glitter to the grafp from afar; and what our great enemy judged a temptation to the humility of a Saviour, muft furely be a certain bait to the ambition of a man.

Oh my poor country, to what art thou devoted! Hadft thou fallen into defpotifm, like many other nations, Hiftory fhould have pitied thee! Hadft thou bowed before the iron rod of an ufurping Tyrant, Memory, while fhe execrated the monfter, would have dropped a tear to the victim! But alas! the hour is come when I fear thou art finking paft redemption: it hath been foretold that thou fhouldft perifh, when thy legiflative became more corrupt than thy executive power—

I did

I did not think the curft prefage would have
been fo cruelly verified, but I dread thou
wilt become the very fcorn of pofterity—
the nation that fell to ruin by having violated
the facred rights of the moft amiable Sovereign that ever graced a throne.

Sir, this may be called mere declamation;
but I truft no honeft man will think fo. I
do flatter myfelf, that in its particular tendency, I have proved this Bill to want that
juftifiable neceffity which alone could warrant
it ; and that, even admitting that to fubfift,
that the Bill is ftill incompetent and inadequate to the evil it profeffes to remedy. The
pedantry of intricate calculation is held out
to carry the appearance of regularity and information ; but, in fact, it only ferves to de-
ter unthinking men from entering on the fubject.—Strip the queftion of all fuperfluous
matter, and we fhall find it to be a weak foe
that cannot long withftand a fteady attack.
I do not by any means feek to decry the Honourable Secretary's algebraical or mathema-
tical talents ; on the contrary, I would make
men cautious by extolling them. I, therefore, allow him all the abilities of *Archi-*
medes ;

medes; and more, I fay he hath advantages peculiar to himfelf. That great man, as hiftory informs us, invented a machine by which he could move this world at his pleafure;— but the globe was preferved becaufe he could find no place to fix his engine on. The Honourable Secretary hath obviated that obftacle to the purpofe he feems to have in view, —overturning this country; and having found a fpot capacious enough to contain his apparatus, let Britain guard in time againft this dreadful machine of patronage, undue influence, and corruption.

THE END.